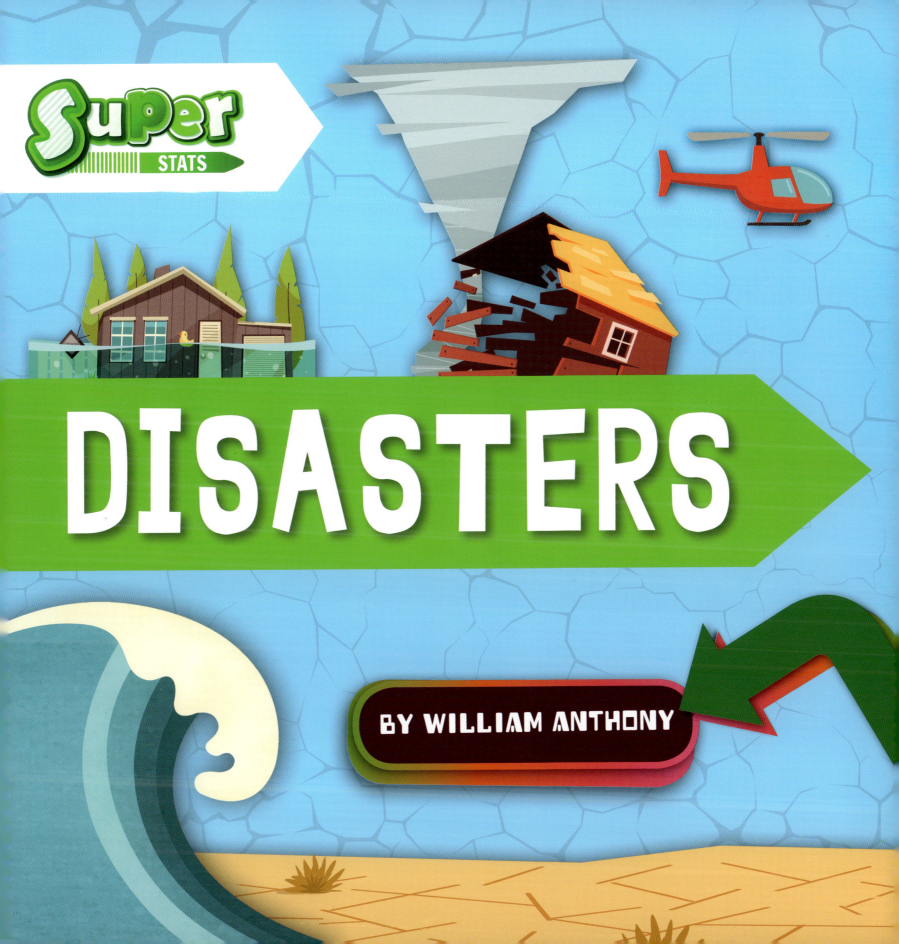

Super STATS

DISASTERS

BY WILLIAM ANTHONY

BookLife
PUBLISHING

©2019
BookLife Publishing Ltd.
King's Lynn
Norfolk, PE30 4LS

ISBN: 978-1-78637-862-0

Written by:
William Anthony

Edited by:
John Wood

Designed by:
Amy Li

A catalogue record for this book is available from the British Library.

All facts, statistics, web addresses and URLs in this book were verified as valid and accurate at time of writing. No responsibility for any changes to external websites or references can be accepted by either the author or publisher.

All rights reserved. Printed in Malaysia.

PHOTO CREDITS

All images courtesy of Shutterstock. With thanks to Getty Images, Thinkstock Photo and iStockphoto

Re-used images (cover & internal) – eakgaraj (background), Olga Milagros (grid), robuart, A.Aleksii (cover graphs), incomible (medals & trophies), Brokso (series logo), Amanita Silvicora (earthquake floor), Arit Fongfung, KIKUCHI (vector people/disaster scenery). Cover – Amanita Silvicora, elenabsl, grimgram, Infinity Eternity, Macrovector, MuchMania, SofiaV, Tancha, VectorPot, ρ1–3 – Tancha, Macrovector, VectorPot, ρ4–5 – Olga1818, Hut Hanna, SofiaV, Infinity Eternity, ρ6–7 – Magicleaf, VectorPot, ρ8–9 – Artur Balytskyi, ρ10–11 – Artur Balytskyi, ProStockStudio, ρ12–13 – ProStockStudio, ρ14–15 – VectoRaith, ρ16–17 – TyBy, Serebrov, ProStockStudio, asantosg, Macrovector, ρ18–19 – Lemberg Vector studio, Visual Generation, avia, Magicleaf, ρ20–21 – vectorpouch, ρ22–23 – Nadya_Art, REANEW, Loveshop, Olga Zelenkova, petch one, Julinzy.

CONTENTS

Words that look like this can be found in the glossary on page 24.

SUPER STATS

Numbers are everywhere. They help us understand lots of different things so we can find out all sorts of information, such as which is the tallest, strongest, biggest or deadliest.

FACT

Stats is short for the word statistics. Statistics are numbers that represent bits of information.

DISASTERS

Our planet can help us to survive, but it can also be deadly. The ground can shake beneath our feet, huge waves and non-stop rain can turn our cities into lakes, and huge mountains can spew fiery lava. These are the <u>natural</u> disasters people around the world may face every day.

TYPES OF DISASTER

Disasters can cause large amounts of damage to our homes and our cities. Disasters can include huge wildfires, strong hurricanes and earthquakes that split the land underneath us.

FACT

A disaster is an event that is so bad that the people of the area need to ask for help.

Some types of disaster happen more often than others. The most common type of disaster in 2018 was flooding. **109** major floods were said to have happened across the planet.

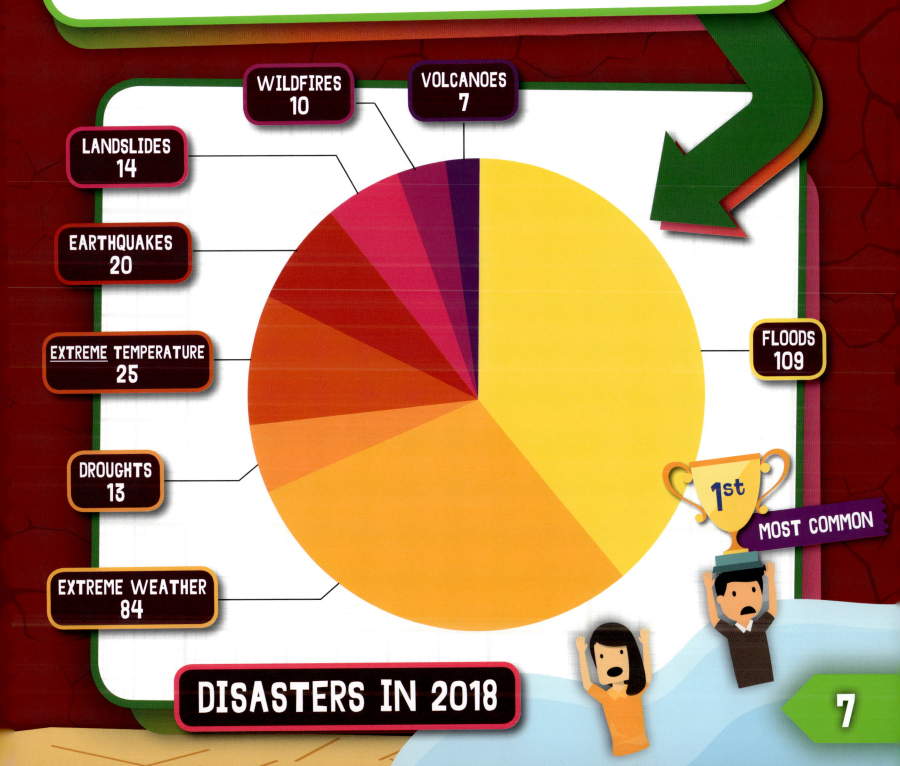

WILDFIRES
10

VOLCANOES
7

LANDSLIDES
14

EARTHQUAKES
20

EXTREME TEMPERATURE
25

FLOODS
109

DROUGHTS
13

EXTREME WEATHER
84

1st

MOST COMMON

DISASTERS IN 2018

BIGGEST EARTHQUAKES

The ground we walk on might seem like it's still, but it is made up of <u>tectonic plates</u> that move very slowly. Sometimes the plates rub up against each other, which can make the ground shake a lot. This is called an earthquake.

STAT ATTACK!

There are **7** main tectonic plates on Earth.

WELCOME

MO'

We can measure how strong an earthquake is by using the Richter scale. The higher the number, the bigger the earthquake and, usually, the greater the damage. The strongest reported earthquake happened in 1960 in Chile. Here's how some other earthquakes <u>compare</u>.

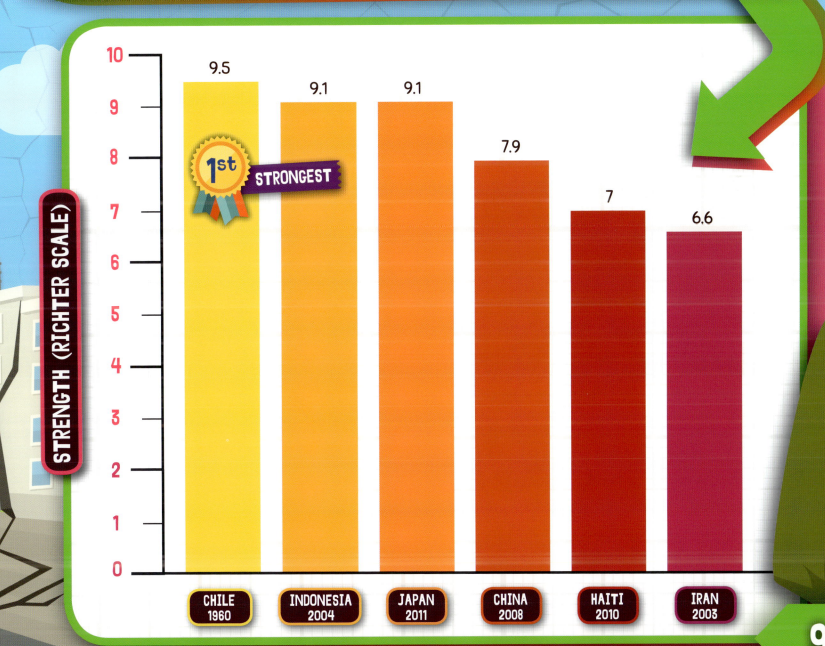

DEADLIEST FLOODS

Sometimes, an earthquake under an ocean can cause a tsunami. A tsunami is a gigantic wave that can destroy cities and create floods. Floods can also be caused by lots and lots of rain over a short time.

STAT ATTACK!

$\frac{1}{6}$ of the homes in England are at risk of flooding.

Floods can be very dangerous. In fact, many people can lose their lives in a flood. The deadliest flood in history happened in 1931 in China. Up to **4 million** people were thought to have died. Here are the deadliest known floods in history:

DEADLIEST 1st

CHINA, 1931
Up to **4 million** people

FACT

The five deadliest known floods in history all took place in China.

CHINA, 1887
Up to **2 million** people

CHINA, 1938
Up to **800,000** people

CHINA, 1975
Up to **230,000** people

CHINA, 1935
Up to **145,000** people

HURRICANES

Hurricanes are a type of <u>tropical storm</u> in the Atlantic and eastern Pacific oceans. Their large, swirling winds are some of the strongest on Earth. They can pick up houses and rip trees out of the ground.

FACT

Tropical storms are each given a name, such as Hurricane Katrina.

When a storm's winds reach **119** kilometres per hour (kph), it is called a hurricane. We can measure how strong a hurricane is by using the Saffir–Simpson scale. The scale uses categories based on how fast the wind speed is.

WIND SPEED (KILOMETRES PER HOUR)

270
250
230
210
190
170
150
130
110

CATEGORY 5
More than 250 kph

CATEGORY 4
210 – 249 kph

CATEGORY 3
178 – 209 kph

CATEGORY 2
154 – 177 kph

CATEGORY 1
119 – 153 kph

DISASTER DEFENCES

Many countries have created defences to prepare for disasters.

JAKARTA

Jakarta is sinking and could flood in the future. To stop this, a wall **40** kilometres long and **24** metres high is being built to block off the ocean.

The Yokohama Landmark Tower in Japan is **296** metres tall. It is built on rollers to stop it wobbling during earthquakes.

Not all disasters come in the form of rumbles in the ground or damaging winds. A disease can be a disaster if it makes lots of people ill very quickly. To protect from diseases, around **85** percent (%) of the world's babies are given <u>vaccines</u>.

BABIES VACCINATED 85%

BABIES NOT VACCINATED 15%

TALLEST VOLCANO

A volcano is an opening in the Earth's <u>crust</u> that spits out fiery lava or ash. It can cause lots of destruction. The tallest volcano in the world is a volcano in Hawaii called Mauna Kea. Over half of the volcano is underwater. From bottom to top it stands at around **10,000** metres tall. Here's how some other things compare.

BURJ KHALIFA

Mauna Kea is taller than **12** Burj Khalifas stacked on top of each other.

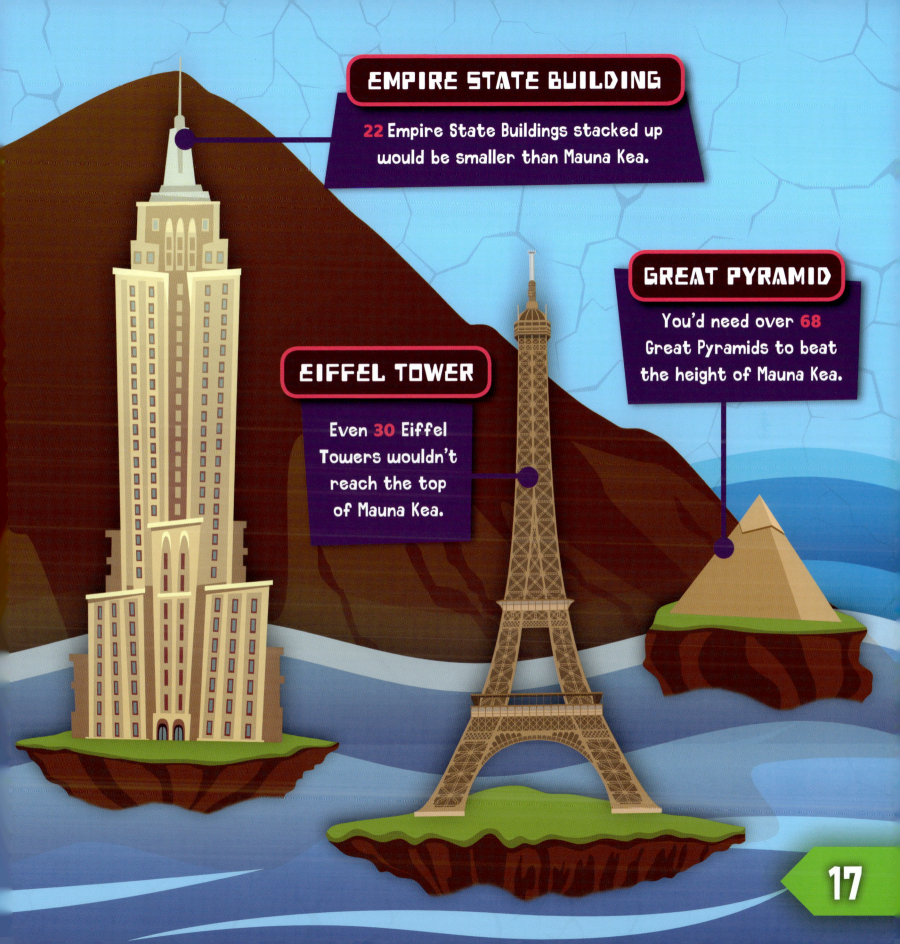

EMPIRE STATE BUILDING

22 Empire State Buildings stacked up would be smaller than Mauna Kea.

EIFFEL TOWER

Even **30** Eiffel Towers wouldn't reach the top of Mauna Kea.

GREAT PYRAMID

You'd need over **68** Great Pyramids to beat the height of Mauna Kea.

COSTLIEST DISASTERS

When a disaster has finished, cities and towns must rebuild. The most damaging disasters can cost a lot of money. Other countries will give <u>resources</u>, called aid, to help the places that suffered from the disaster.

FACT

The US is the biggest donor of aid in the world.

The biggest disasters can cost billions of pounds in damage. The costliest disaster ever was the Japanese earthquake and tsunami of 2011. It cost around **181 billion** British pounds in damage. These are the top five costliest disasters in history.

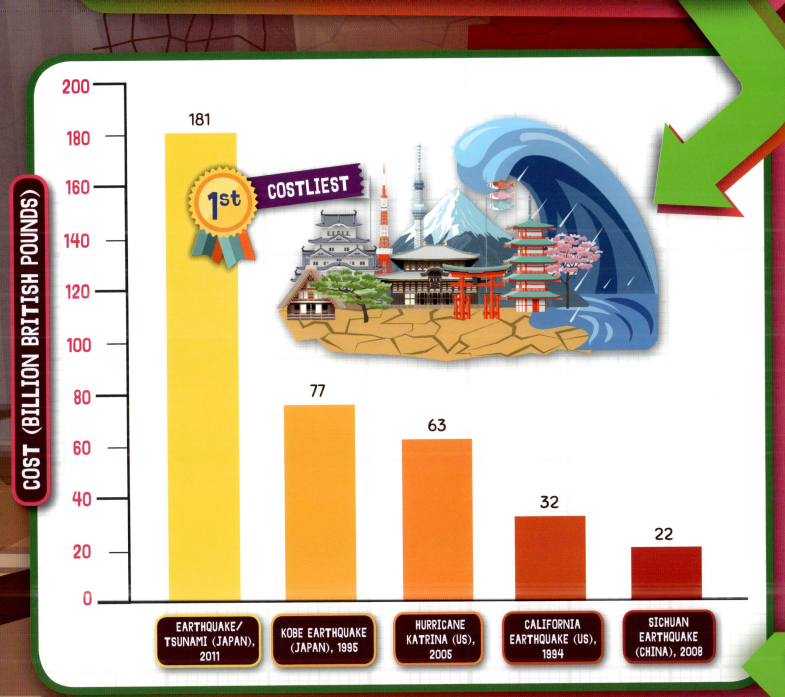

COST (BILLION BRITISH POUNDS)

1st

COSTLIEST

181

77

63

32

22

EARTHQUAKE/ TSUNAMI (JAPAN), 2011

KOBE EARTHQUAKE (JAPAN), 1995

HURRICANE KATRINA (US), 2005

CALIFORNIA EARTHQUAKE (US), 1994

SICHUAN EARTHQUAKE (CHINA), 2008

THE BLACK DEATH

Some disasters are caused by things we can't even see. In the 1300s, a type of <u>bacteria</u> caused a big disaster – the Black Death. The disease caused big black boils, called buboes, to grow under the arms and around the groin.

FACT

The Black Death is another name for the plague.

The disease usually ended in death. Across the whole of Europe, the Black Death is thought to have killed around **25 million** people. Some historians think that it may have wiped out around **1 in 3** people in Europe.

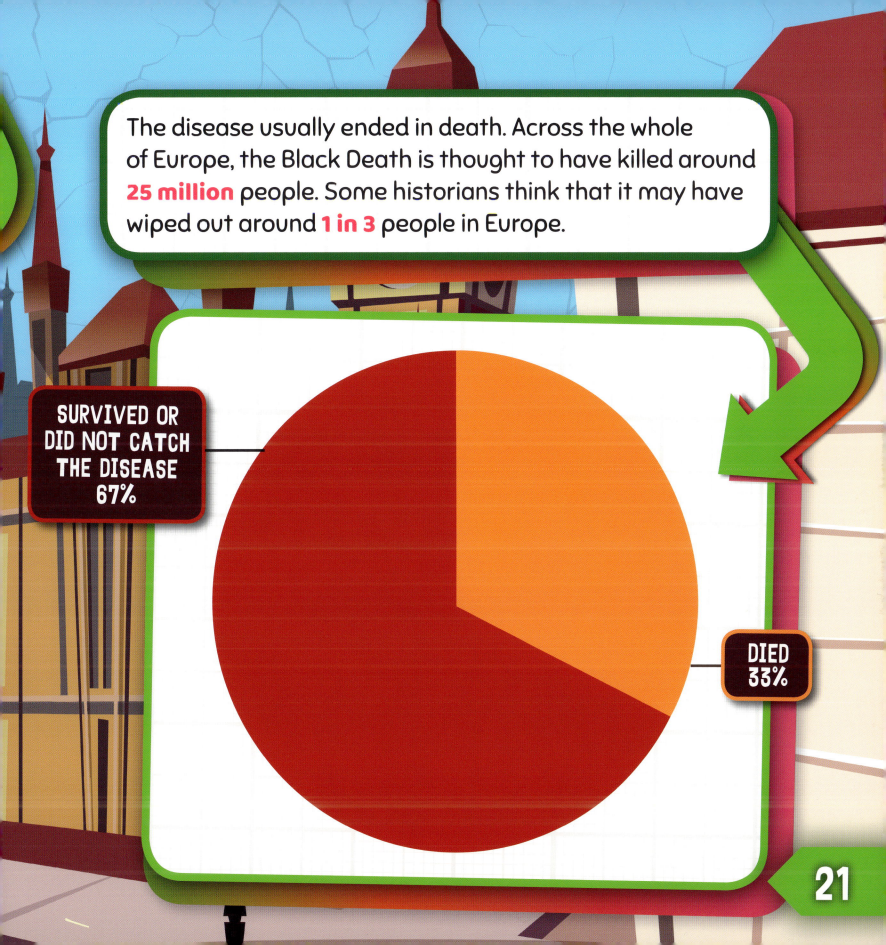

SURVIVED OR DID NOT CATCH THE DISEASE 67%

DIED 33%

BIGGEST ASTEROID HIT

Disasters can come from anywhere – even space. Asteroids are huge rocky objects in space. Sometimes, these large rocks can crash into planets such as Earth. When something so big hits our planet, it leaves something called a crater in the ground.

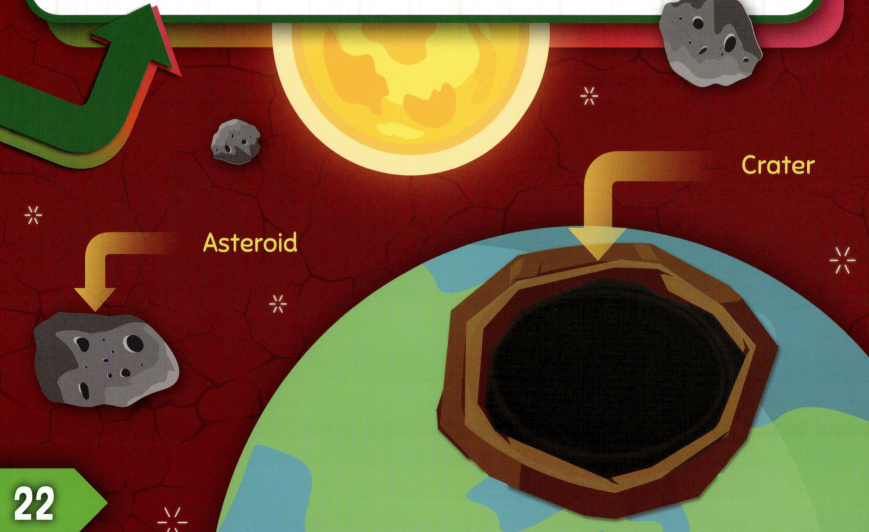

Asteroid

Crater

The biggest asteroid to hit Earth landed southwest of what is now Johannesburg, South Africa, around **2 billion** years ago. It made the Vredefort Crater, which is so big that all of these countries put together could fit inside...

BELGIUM

JAMAICA

ISRAEL

ANDORRA

LUXEMBOURG

SINGAPORE

BARBADOS

GLOSSARY

bacteria	tiny living things, too small to see, that can cause diseases
compare	to look at two or more things to see what is similar or different about them
crust	the hard, outermost layer of the Earth
extreme	much beyond what is normal or expected
natural	found in nature and not made by humans
resources	supplies of money, materials, food, water or people
tectonic plates	the large, hard, moving pieces of rock that make up the outer surface of the Earth
tropical storm	a very strong, swirling wind system that forms over warm, tropical oceans
vaccines	things that are usually injected into a person to protect against a disease

INDEX